The Chocolate Trail

Julie Haydon

Contents

Rigby®

P9-DEL-964

Editor's Letter

Welcome to *The Chocolate Trail* — the magazine for chocolate lovers! Chocolate is a delicious treat that most people love eating and drinking. But who discovered chocolate? What is it made of? How is it made?

To find the answers to these tantalizing questions, follow our reporters as they set off along the chocolate trail.

Dee Lishus

EDITOR

Chocolate doesn't grow on trees, but cocoa beans do! Chocolate is made from cocoa beans.

Cocoa beans are the seeds of the cacao tree. They grow inside pods on cacao trees.

cacao tree

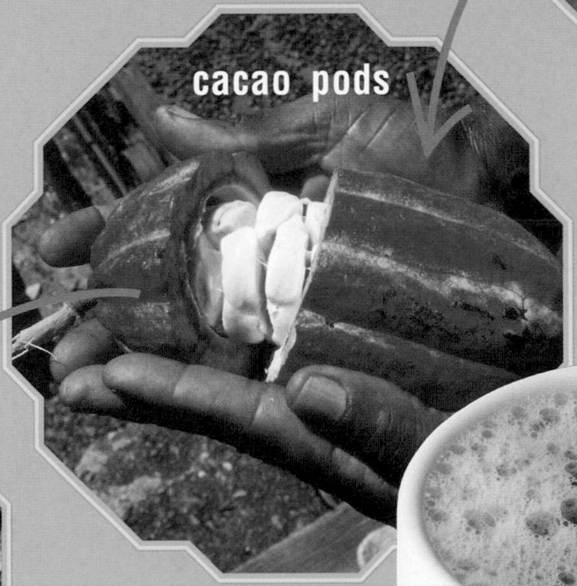

cacao pods

cocoa beans

chocolate

late trail

Discovering
Chocolate

Ancient Peoples Drink Chocolate

by B. Itter

LONG AGO, the ancient **Maya** and **Aztecs** made chocolate drinks from cocoa beans. They collected the beans from the cacao trees that grew on plantations in Central America and southern Mexico.

They dried, roasted, and crushed the cocoa beans, then mixed them with water. The chocolate drinks were flavored with ingredients such as chili peppers and vanilla.

Love That Foam!

by K. Reemy

THE MAYA AND AZTECS liked their chocolate drinks topped with foam. They thought the foam was the best part of the drink. To make the foam, they held a jar full of chocolate up high and then poured the chocolate into another jar below. Sometimes they added cornmeal to the chocolate. Then they beat the mixture to make foam.

The first chocolate drinks were bitter and spicy and made with water, not milk. The Maya and Aztecs did not have sugar.

A cocoa plantation

Growing Money on Trees

by Chuck Latt

CHOCOLATE was very important to the Maya and Aztecs. They planted cacao trees and then harvested the cocoa beans, so they could make chocolate. These were the first cocoa plantations.

Chocolate was a drink mostly for the rich and powerful. Cocoa beans were valuable and also used as money. People could trade cocoa beans for just about anything, such as cooking pots, food, and clothes.

Columbus Sees Cocoa Beans

by Tay Stee

THE EXPLORER Christopher Columbus was one of the first Europeans to see cocoa beans. On a voyage to Central America in 1502, he met some native people in a large canoe. The canoe held various trading goods, including cocoa beans. Columbus thought the beans were a type of almond.

Although Christopher Columbus was one of the first Europeans to see cocoa beans, he never tasted chocolate!

Chocolate in Europe

Chocolate Arrives in Europe

by B. Itter

IN THE 1500s, the Spanish conquered Central America, Mexico, and parts of South America. As a result, many native goods, including cocoa beans, were shipped to Spain. Chocolate had arrived in Europe!

Over time, chocolate became a favorite drink of the rich and powerful in Spain. They added sugar to the chocolate to make it sweet.

Cocoa beans were expensive and rare, so chocolate was not a common drink. It was many **decades** before other countries in Europe learned the recipe for chocolate. It took even longer for chocolate to reach North America.

When Europeans realized how valuable cocoa beans were, they started their own cocoa plantations. Cacao trees only grow well in warm, **humid** conditions, so plantations are found in **tropical** countries near the **equator**.

Cacao trees

Eating Chocolate

A Treat to Eat

by N. R. Gee

BY THE LATE 1600s, people had begun using chocolate in desserts and other dishes. Soon, chocolate was being added to sorbets, cakes, and even some meat dishes!

Chocolate bars were made in England in 1847. The chocolate was dark and bitter, but the bars were very popular.

Milk chocolate was invented in Switzerland in the 1870s. It was made with powdered milk, not fresh milk.

In some European cities, people used to meet in special cafes called chocolate houses. People spent many hours at these cafes drinking chocolate and talking with their friends.

Cacao Trees

The Business of Chocolate

by K. Reemy

TODAY, chocolate is big business. Cacao trees are grown on small family farms and on large plantations in many tropical countries. Cacao trees are often planted with other taller trees. These taller trees give shade and attract **pollinating** insects.

The cacao pods grow on the trunks or branches of the cacao trees. The pods are shaped like melons. When the pods are ripe, they are yellow, orange, or red. Inside the pods are 30 to 40 cocoa beans surrounded by a fleshy, white pulp.

Raw cocoa beans are usually purple or white.

Harvesting the Beans

by S. Weet

CACAO PODS are usually harvested twice a year. Workers cut the pods from the trees with large knives. They have to be careful not to damage the trees. The pods are then cut open, and the pulp and beans are taken out.

Cutting a pod from a cacao tree

The pulp and beans are piled up on the ground or put in boxes. They are covered and left in the sun to **ferment**. Fermentation brings out the chocolate flavor in the beans.

The pulp turns to liquid and drains away.

The cocoa beans are dried in the sun or in large dryers. Then, they are packed in sacks, ready to go to a factory.

Wild animals, such as monkeys, squirrels, and rats, will open cacao pods and eat the juicy, white pulp. They do not eat the bitter beans.

Cocoa beans drying in the sun

At the Factory

Chocolate's Most Important Ingredient

by Tay Stee

Roasted cocoa beans

COCOA MASS is the most important ingredient in chocolate. It is a paste made from cocoa beans. Cocoa mass is made at a factory.

First, the cocoa beans are sorted, cleaned, and roasted. (Roasting the beans brings out more of the chocolate flavor.) Then the shells are removed. The parts of the beans that are left are called **nibs**. The nibs are ground to make cocoa mass.

Cocoa mass is thick and bitter.

Making Cocoa Powder

by Chuck Latt

COCOA POWDER is used to make chocolate drinks and chocolate flavoring. To make cocoa powder, some of the fat in the cocoa mass must be removed. This fat is called cocoa butter.

The cocoa mass is pressed in large machines. This squeezes out some of the cocoa butter. A solid block of cocoa is left, and it is ground into cocoa powder.

Cocoa powder

Making Chocolate

A conching machine

Chocolate to Eat

by N. R. Gee

PLAIN chocolate is dark. It is made from cocoa mass, cocoa butter, and sugar.

The ingredients are mixed together to make a paste. The paste is ground so that it is smooth. The paste goes into a **conching machine** where it is mixed and beaten for hours, turning it into liquid chocolate. Then, the chocolate is carefully cooled.

The chocolate is now ready to be made into products.

Milk chocolate is made in the same way as plain chocolate, but milk is added to the recipe.

Chocolate, Chocolate Everywhere

by Chuck Latt

HAVE you ever wondered how blocks and bars of chocolate are made?

Blocks of chocolate are made in molds. Liquid chocolate is poured into the molds. Sometimes other ingredients, such as nuts and fruit, are added. The molds are cooled and the chocolate hardens. The solid blocks of chocolate are tipped out of the molds and wrapped.

Chocolate bars have fillings under the chocolate. The filling is mixed and cooked.

Then it is cooled and cut to size. The pieces of filling are then coated with chocolate. (The bottom of the bar is covered with chocolate first, then the top and sides.) After the chocolate sets, the bars are wrapped and packaged.

Molds holding liquid chocolate are **vibrated** to get rid of air bubbles.

Solid blocks of chocolate

Ask the Editor

Q. What is white chocolate made of?

A. White chocolate is made with cocoa butter, sugar, and milk. Some people do not think white chocolate is really chocolate because it is not made with cocoa mass.

Q. What are other names for cocoa beans?

A. Cacao beans or cacao seeds

Q. Did early native peoples in South America make chocolate?

A. There's no proof they did. However, they collected cacao pods and ate the fleshy pulp.

Q. Why do soldiers, hikers, and athletes often carry chocolate bars?

A. Chocolate is high in fat and sugar. This makes chocolate a good food to eat when you need an energy boost.

Glossary

Aztecs ancient people of central Mexico

cocoa mass a paste made from ground cocoa bean nibs

conching machine a machine that mixes and beats liquid chocolate to make it smooth

decades groups of ten years

equator the imaginary line around the Earth that divides it into two hemispheres

ferment to break down and produce a chemical change

humid moist air

Maya ancient people of Central America and southern Mexico

nibs the insides or centers of cocoa beans

pollinating to cause a plant to make seeds by sprinkling it with tiny grains called pollen

tropical warm and frost-free

vibrated shaken quickly

Index